A STROLL THROUGH OLD CARDIFF

Views from my Postcard Collection

PETER BEST

Sou'wester Books

For my late parents

Copyright © Peter Best/Sou'wester Books 1992

ISBN 0 9515281 5 7

Published by Sou'wester Books, 17 Crestacre Close,
Newton, Swansea SA3 4UR

Printed by W. Walters, Son & Co. Ltd., Clydach, Swansea.

INTRODUCTION

Looking for a relaxation from business, and having a long-standing interest in his home town, Peter Best began to renew his earlier interest in picture postcard collecting about twenty years ago. Though still a keen collector of postcards of old Cardiff, he also runs a part-time business as a dealer in postcards.

The collection he has built up is the basis for this fascinating glimpse of the city streets and its people in the early years of the century. Picture postcard production was then big business and the collection of cards became a popular pastime. Sadly many of the collections have ended in the dustbin, but sufficient have survived to help us discover the city of our grandparents.

The cards reproduced here are the work of many different publishers - a few local to Cardiff others, such as Valentine, being national concerns. The photographers in general are unknown, though the best street scenes in this collection are the work of Ernest Bush of the Royal Photographic Company.

The author, who is chairman of the South Wales Postcard Club, has shown his collection to many clubs and societies as slides. Let him now take you for a stroll through the streets of old Cardiff, and then catch a tram or horse bus for home.

ACKNOWLEDGEMENTS

The publisher wishes to thank Lin Bryant of Pencoed for his interest and assistance; Bryn Jones, Local Studies Librarian at South Glamorgan County Library, for his help in identifying some of the views; and Dennis Pope of Pope's Photo Service who produced the copies of the original postcards.

4   A STROLL THROUGH OLD CARDIFF

Photographer Ernest Bush took this view looking south east from the castle clock tower. Electric trams turn the Castle Street/High Street corner while outside the castle a lady alights from the Llandaff horse bus.

Queen Street at its junction with St John Street. This photograph was taken in about 1900 before the introduction of the electric trams.

A STROLL THROUGH OLD CARDIFF

Queen Street. This view was taken about ten years after the last. The electric trams have arrived and there are many new buildings.

The Carlton Restaurant in Queen Street was opened in 1914. Previous pages show that the right hand sections of the building were an extension.

A STROLL THROUGH OLD CARDIFF

This view of Queen Street during the First World War was taken by Ernest Bush of the Royal Photographic Company.

St John's Church. Another fine view by Ernest Bush.

Church Street. The tower of St John's was completed in 1473. Oliver's on the corner was the biggest retailer of shoes in the world.

Looking north from the tower of St John's Church.

The castle north lodge alongside the Glamorganshire Canal. The building was destroyed by incendiary bombs in March 1941.

Duke Street viewed from Castle Street. The buildings on the north side (the left) backed straight on to the castle wall and were demolished in 1923 to make a modern thoroughfare accessible to traffic.

Duke Street from Queen Street. Notice the Green Dragon restaurant on the left and the Duke St Arcade. On the right is Marments.

Duke Street after widening.

A STROLL THROUGH OLD CARDIFF 15

Schoolchildren enter the castle grounds in the Corpus Christi procession in 1911.

"Cardiff: City of Arcades." The Royal Arcade was built in 1856.

A STROLL THROUGH OLD CARDIFF

Teddy Morgan scored the winning try in the famous but controversial match against the All Blacks in 1905.

The Angel Hotel, on the corner of Castle and Westgate Streets, has seen many a celebration after rugby internationals at the Arms Park.

20 A STROLL THROUGH OLD CARDIFF

The City Hall. On the right is the memorial to Welshmen who died in the South African (Boer) War.

The Lord Mayor and members of the first City Council, 23 October 1905.

The General Post Office in Westgate Street.

The library in The Hayes. The statue is of John Batchelor, shipbuilder and timber merchant, better known as "The Friend of Freedom" for his radical views.

The city fire brigade in the station yard next door to the old town hall in St Mary Street. The appliances to left and right had steam pumps but were horse drawn. The appliance at centre was the brigade's pride and joy - The King a Merryweather power driven fire engine.

St Mary Street. The Great Western Hotel and Western Mail building on the left. The Bute statue has been moved across the road but the scene is otherwise little changed today.

A STROLL THROUGH OLD CARDIFF

26 A STROLL THROUGH OLD CARDIFF

The Glamorganshire Canal emerges from the tunnel and passes under the railway bridge near Cardiff General station. The Custom House and York Hotel are on the left and Central Hotel on the right.

The triumphal arch erected across Bute Street for the visit of King Edward VII and Queen Alexandra in July 1907. During the visit the Queen Alexandra dock was officially opened.

28 A STROLL THROUGH OLD CARDIFF

Sail and steam in the Bute Docks. This view is of the rather narrow west dock and entrance basin. On the right a ship can be seen in the Junction Dry Dock. The east dock is in the distance on the right of the picture.

Coal hoists at the Queen Alexandra Dock.

Cardiff Docks and S.S. Westonia and S.S. Gwalia.

30 A STROLL THROUGH OLD CARDIFF

Taken in 1905 this card shows the paddle steamers Westonia and Gwalia of the Red Funnel fleet. In summer their decks were crowded with trippers off to Weston or Ilfracombe.

Catching up with news or enjoying a game of draughts at the John Cory Sailors' and Soldiers' Rest at 179-80 Bute Street.

Staff and patients of the male surgical ward of the Royal Hamadryad Hospital.

The Y.M.C.A. building in Station Terrace.

34 A STROLL THROUGH OLD CARDIFF

The Royal Infirmary was opened in 1883.

This operating theatre at the Royal Infirmary was opened in 1901.

36 A STROLL THROUGH OLD CARDIFF

Newport Road. In the early years of the century it was still known as Roath Road.

Albany Road, Roath.

38 A STROLL THROUGH OLD CARDIFF

The junction of Albany and Marlborough Roads.

Clifton Street.

Splott Road.

Roath Road Methodist Chapel in Newport Road was badly damaged by enemy bombing in March 1941 and demolished in 1955.

42 A STROLL THROUGH OLD CARDIFF

The Clarence Bridge was opened by the Duke of Clarence in 1890 and replaced by the present bridge in 1976.

Fitzhamon Embankment, Riverside.

Plasturton Avenue, Cardiff. No. 1264.

44 A STROLL THROUGH OLD CARDIFF

Plasturton Avenue took its name from the farm, part of the Bute estate, on which it was built.

The largest load transported by road in the city. The boiler and transporter stand outside Frank's confectionery works.

46 A STROLL THROUGH OLD CARDIFF

Cathedral Road was a leafy residential area in the early years of the century.

Cowbridge Road looking west from the junction with Clive Road. The chimney of Ely paper mill is in the distance.

A STROLL THROUGH OLD CARDIFF 47

48 A STROLL THROUGH OLD CARDIFF

Cowbridge Road at its junction with Llandaff Road. A tram picks up passengers for the city centre.

Ely bridge and breweries.

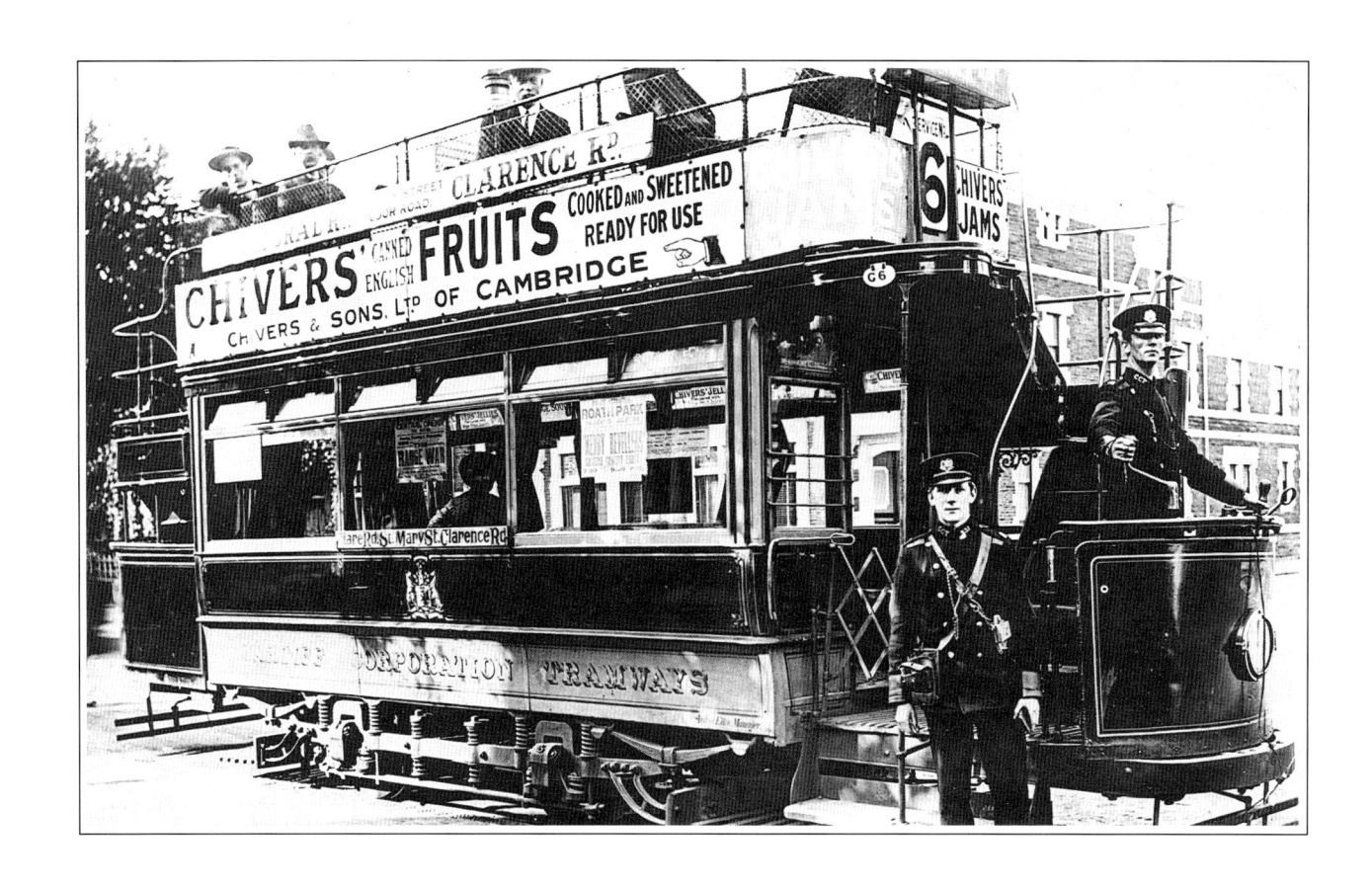

The electric trams were a feature of the city streets for almost fifty years. This open top double decker was introduced in 1902.

Newport Road during the First World War.

52   A STROLL THROUGH OLD CARDIFF

The crowd enjoys the band on a summer day at Roath Park. The 100 acre park was opened by the Earl of Dumfries on his 13th birthday in June 1894.

The aquarium at Roath Park.

A STROLL THROUGH OLD CARDIFF 53

Whitchurch. The Plough hotel on the left. The solid tyre bus carries an advert "Templar Malins for teeth, 51 Queen St."

54 A STROLL THROUGH OLD CARDIFF

Great excitement as the balloon Willows II flies over Pen y Lan in June 1910. The airship, designed and built by 24 year old E.T. Willows of Cardiff, was flown in August that year from East Moors to Crystal Palace, London.

A STROLL THROUGH OLD CARDIFF

A STROLL THROUGH OLD CARDIFF

A moment for reflection at Thompson Park.

Howard Gardens. The statue is of Henry Austin Bruce, Lord Aberdare, Home Secretary from 1868 to 73.

Building the garden village suburb of Rhiwbina.

OLD CHURCH RADYR.

A tranquil scene at Radyr.

60 A STROLL THROUGH OLD CARDIFF

The Cow and Snuffers public house alongside a lock on the Glamorganshire Canal at Llandaff.